WEATHER IN 30 SECONDS

First published in the UK in 2015 by Ivy Kids.
This edition published in the US in 2017 by

Ivy Kids

Ovest House
58 West Street
Brighton BN1 2RA
United Kingdom
www.quartoknows.com

A CIP record for this book is available from the Library of Congress.

ISBN: 978-1-78240-488-0

This book was conceived, designed & produced by

Ivy Kids

PUBLISHER Susan Kelly
CREATIVE DIRECTOR Michael Whitehead
COMMISSIONING EDITOR Hazel Songhurst
MANAGING EDITOR Susie Behar
PROJECT EDITOR Cath Senker
ART DIRECTOR Kim Hankinson
DESIGNER Hanri Shaw
DESIGN ASSISTANT Emily Hurlock
EDITORIAL ASSISTANT Lucy Menzies

Printed in China

10 9 8 7 6 5 4 3 2 1

WEATHER
IN 30 SECONDS

DR JEN GREEN

ILLUSTRATED BY TOM WOOLLEY
CONSULTANT: PROFESSOR ADAM SCAIFE

IVY KIDS

Contents

About this book

... in 60 seconds

Before you begin this book, find out what is happening outside. Is the air warm, stifling hot, or icy? Is it calm or breezy? It may be sunny or cloudy—or perhaps rain, sleet, or snow is falling. All these conditions describe the weather—the state of the atmosphere at a given place and time.

In some parts of the world, the weather stays the same for days or even weeks. But in many places it changes constantly, as storm clouds move in to cover a blue sky, or the sun peeps through after rain. Ever-changing weather keeps us guessing, and even the climate, which is the general weather for a region measured over many years, is slowly changing.

Weather affects each and every one of us every day. It affects where we live and how we travel, the clothes we wear and what we do. We also rely on weather to grow our food. This book will explore the many faces of weather and climate. It will explain the awesome forces behind weather systems and describe all the different types of weather that affect us around the globe.

From hailstones to hurricanes, the weather seems to be getting wilder. Scientists believe this is because the climate is changing rapidly. We'll examine why this is happening and what it might mean for the future.

This book explores 30 weather topics, arranged in six chapters. Each topic has a page that explains the basics in 30 seconds. If that's too long, a 3-second summary gives you the key points. Three-minute missions throughout the book explore the science behind the weather. In this book you will experience the full force of the elements, so grab your sun hat, jacket, and boots and get ready for a whistle-stop tour of the world's wild and wonderful weather!

Earth's weather

You may be surprised to hear that all weather on Earth is caused by moving air, stirred up by the Sun's energy. This simple-sounding process gives rise to awesome weather systems such as gales, thunderstorms, and tornadoes. The energy created by weather is so powerful that it can sometimes be used to drive machinery. This chapter explains the source of energy and the forces that interact to produce the weather from the Sun, the atmosphere, and the oceans.

Earth's weather
Glossary

air pressure The weight of the air in the atmosphere that presses down toward earth.

Antarctic The region of the world around the South Pole.

Arctic The region of the world around the North Pole.

atmosphere The mixture of gases that surrounds Earth.

axis An imaginary line through the center of Earth, around which the planet turns.

continent One of the large land masses of Earth, such as Europe, Asia, or Africa.

current The movement of air or water in a particular direction.

Equator An imaginary horizontal line around the middle of Earth.

fossil fuel A fuel, such as coal or oil, that was formed over millions of years from the remains of animals or plants.

gravity The force that attracts objects toward each other and that pulls objects on Earth toward the center of the planet. This is why things fall to the ground when they are dropped.

gyre A large system of circulating ocean currents formed by global wind patterns and forces created by Earth's rotation.

hurricane A violent storm with strong winds, especially occurring over the western Atlantic Ocean.

hydroelectric power A form of power that uses water to produce electricity.

nuclear reaction A process in which the nuclei (the cores at the center of atoms) release a huge amount of energy.

pollution When dirty or harmful substances are added to land, air, or water so that it is no longer safe or pleasant to use.

pressure The amount of force that acts over a particular area.

radiate To give off energy as heat or light.

renewable energy Energy that is replaced naturally so it can be used without the risk of using it all up.

solar panel A piece of equipment that uses light from the Sun to produce hot water and electricity.

solar power Turning heat and light from the Sun's rays into energy that people can use.

temperate Having mild temperatures, which are never very hot or very cold.

tide The regular rise and fall in the level of the sea, caused by the pull of the Moon and the rotation of Earth.

tropical Coming from, found in, or typical of the tropics.

tropics The area just above and below the Equator. The climate is warm and hot, and moist all year round.

troposphere The lowest layer of Earth's atmosphere where weather occurs, up to about 5 to 10 miles (about 8 to 16 km) above the surface.

turbine A machine or an engine that receives its power from a wheel that is turned by the pressure of water, air, or gas.

water vapor Water in the form of a gas.

11

The Sun

...in 30 seconds

Our nearest star, the Sun, is an enormous ball of burning gases. Deep in the Sun's core, continuous nuclear reactions release vast amounts of energy so that light and heat radiate out in all directions. This is the main source of energy for weather on Earth.

The Sun is so huge that over a million Earths would fit inside it! Its vast mass produces gravity, which keeps Earth and other planets circling around it. Earth is 93 million miles (150 million km) from the Sun—just the right distance for temperatures to be comfortable and for life to flourish.

Because Earth is round, the Sun heats its surface unevenly. The Equator is facing the Sun so it gets the strongest rays. This produces a warm, sunny climate all year round—lovely! Where Earth curves away toward the Poles, it is facing away from the Sun. Here, the Sun is always low in the sky, and fewer rays hit the surface so it is not heated as much.

These differences give us three main temperature zones on Earth: hot tropical regions, icy polar regions, and mild (temperate) regions in between.

3-second sum-up

The Sun provides the energy that drives weather.

3-minute mission Test the Sun's heating power

You need: • 2 pieces of cardboard • Books to prop up cardboard • Masking tape • 2 thermometers

Tape a thermometer to each piece of cardboard. Place both pieces where they will receive sunlight for 30 minutes. Tilt one piece so the thermometer directly faces the Sun. Place the other one flat so it receives indirect sunlight. Record the temperatures every two minutes until they stop rising. The cardboard tilted toward the Sun should be hotter. This is because the sunlight struck it directly, just as the Sun's rays strike Earth near the Equator.

The Sun heats Earth most at the Equator and least at the Poles.

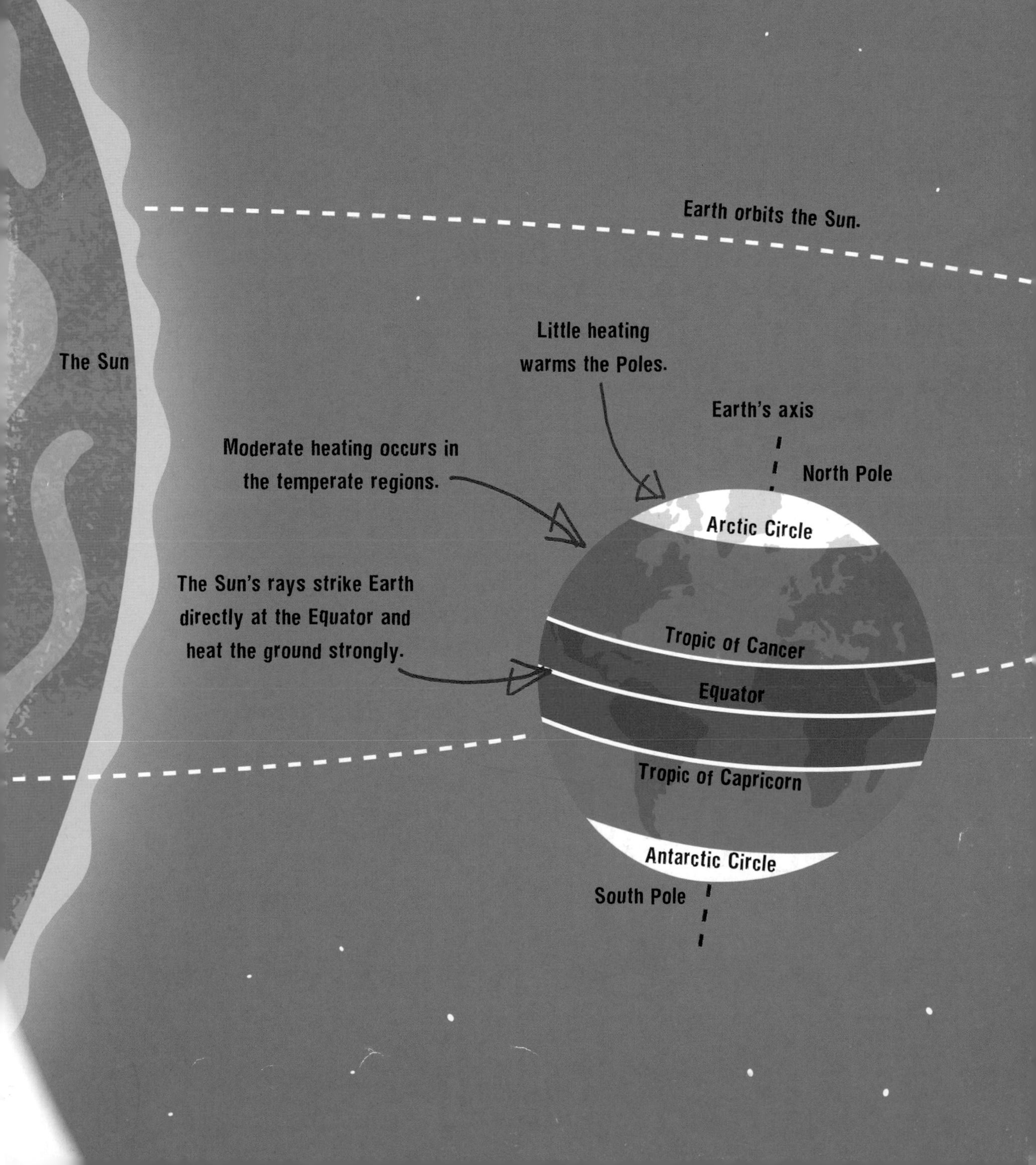

Earth orbits the Sun.

Little heating warms the Poles.

The Sun

Moderate heating occurs in the temperate regions.

The Sun's rays strike Earth directly at the Equator and heat the ground strongly.

Earth's axis

North Pole

Arctic Circle

Tropic of Cancer

Equator

Tropic of Capricorn

Antarctic Circle

South Pole

The atmosphere

...in 30 seconds

Surrounding our planet is a blanket of gas, which is called the atmosphere. This thin layer dilutes the Sun's heat, making conditions comfortable for us. Without the atmosphere, there would be no weather and Earth's surface would be silent like the Moon.

The air in our atmosphere is made up of two main gases. About four-fifths of the air is nitrogen and about a fifth is oxygen. There are also traces of other gases, such as carbon dioxide, argon, and water vapor.

Earth's atmosphere stretches about 6,200 miles (10,000 km) toward space and is made up of five main layers—99.9 percent of the air is within just 30 miles (50 km) of the surface. The bottom layer, the troposphere, contains more than 75 percent of the air and 99 percent of the moisture. This layer is also where weather events occur, but the swirling air makes conditions bumpy for aircraft, which is why planes fly above the clouds and weather systems.

The weight of the air produces a force called air pressure. Air pressure is greatest at sea level because this layer feels the weight of all the air above. Higher up, the air is thinner, so each breath you take contains less oxygen. That's why mountain climbers use bottled oxygen to climb the world's highest peaks.

3-second sum-up

The atmosphere is made up of a thin layer of gases around Earth.

3-minute mission Test air pressure

You need: • Plastic cup, one-third full of water • Piece of cardboard

Cover the cup with the cardboard. Take the cup to a sink and turn it upside down, holding the piece of cardboard firmly against the cup. Take your hand away from the cardboard—the water stays in the upside-down cup! The air pressure is greater around the cup than inside it, and this prevents the water from pouring out.

Earth's atmosphere is made up of five thin layers.

Exosphere

Thermosphere

Mesosphere

Stratosphere

Troposphere

Passenger jets fly above the clouds and weather systems.

The bright lights of auroras shine in the thermosphere.

Meteors from space burn up in the mesosphere.

Satellites circle Earth in the exosphere.

Weather balloons collect weather data up in the stratosphere.

Weather happens in the troposphere.

A space rocket exits Earth's atmosphere.

Oceans and seas
...in 30 seconds

We live on a watery planet—more than two-thirds of Earth's surface is covered by oceans and seas. So it's hardly surprising that water has a big effect on the world's weather. Oceans and seas store heat energy from the Sun and help to spread it around the globe.

The Sun heats the oceans unevenly. Tropical waters near the Equator are warm while polar seas are cold and mostly ice-covered. However, ocean water is constantly being stirred by waves, tides, and currents that help to spread the Sun's heat.

Currents flow around the world in huge circles called gyres, which are caused by the shape of the continents. Warm currents from the tropics drift toward the Poles, heating the lands they flow past. Cold polar currents flow back toward the Equator, cooling the lands they flow past.

The oceans warm more slowly than the land as they absorb the Sun's rays. They also release heat more slowly. This makes the oceans cooler than the land in summer and warmer in winter. That's why the middle of a continent is hotter in summer and colder in winter than land by the coast.

3-second sum-up

Oceans help to spread heat from the Sun around the globe.

3-minute mission Sun, land, and sea

You need: • 2 thermometers • Jar of soil • Jar of water

1 Fill one jar with soil and the other with water to represent the land and the oceans. Stick a thermometer in each jar.

2 Place both jars in the sunshine for an hour and then record the temperatures.

3 Move the jars into the fridge for an hour and take the temperatures again. You should find that the soil heats up and also loses heat more quickly than the water.

Warm and cold currents of water flow around the world, affecting the weather.

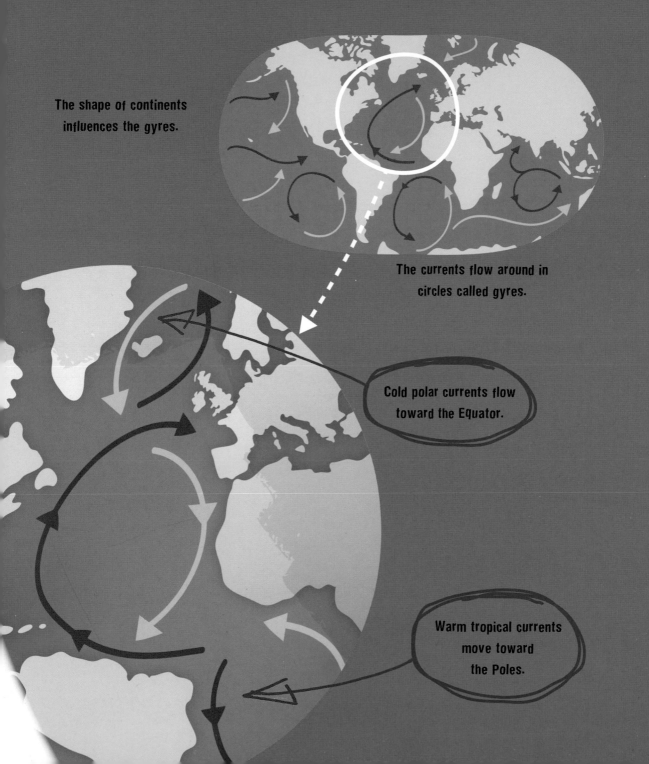

The shape of continents influences the gyres.

The currents flow around in circles called gyres.

Cold polar currents flow toward the Equator.

Warm tropical currents move toward the Poles.

Winds

...in 30 seconds

Winds are air on the move. From a gentle breeze to a howling gale, all winds are caused by one thing—differences in air pressure.

When the Sun shines on the sea or the land, the energy is absorbed and warms the air above. Warm air is less dense than cold air and so it rises. This creates an area of low pressure. Cooler air rushes into the place where air has risen, producing wind. Air always tries to move from an area of high pressure to one of low pressure. It's like letting air out of a balloon.

You can't see the wind but you can measure it in two ways: by strength (wind speed) and by direction. Winds are named after the direction they are blowing from, so a northerly breeze blows from the north toward the south.

In most parts of the world, the wind mainly blows from one direction—this is called a prevailing wind. Warm air rises near the Equator and flows toward the Poles where it cools, sinks, and flows back toward the Equator. Yet most winds don't flow directly from north to south because they are also bent by Earth's rotation. This bending is named the Coriolis Effect.

3-second sum-up

Winds are currents of moving air that can be measured in strength and direction.

The Beaufort Scale

In the early 19th century, a British naval officer, Sir Francis Beaufort, invented a scale to measure wind. The Beaufort Scale is a 12-point scale, where 0 is dead calm and 12 is a violent hurricane. The scale proved so useful that we still use it today.

The Beaufort Scale measures wind strengths, ranging from dead calm at 0 to a raging hurricane at 12.

0 Calm
Wind speed: Less than 1 mph (1 kph)   Sea flat like a mirror

3 Gentle breeze
Wind speed: 8–12 mph (12–19 kph)   Wavelets; crests begin to form

5 Fresh breeze
Wind speed: 19–24 mph (29–38 kph)   Moderate waves; small trees sway

7 Near gale
Wind speed: 32–38 mph (50–61 kph)   Sea builds up; whole trees move

10 Storm
Wind speed: 55–63 mph (89–102 kph)   Extremely high waves; trees uproot

12 Hurricane
Wind speed: 73 mph
(118 kph) or higher   Violence and destruction

Weather power

...in 30 seconds

The energy that creates our weather also provides useful energy for light, heating, cooking, and driving machinery. People have been using the power of the wind and moving water for centuries.

In the past, windmills used wind power to grind grain. Flowing water from rivers fed by rainfall powered water wheels. Today, you can see wind turbines spinning in the breeze to produce electricity. Hydroelectric plants use flowing water to make electricity. We have also learned how to capture the energy of waves and tides.

We can use energy from the Sun directly, too. Solar power plants convert sunlight into electricity. People can have their own solar panels on the roof. And did you know that small devices such as flashlights, calculators, and cell phones can also run on solar energy?

For centuries, people have mainly relied on fossil fuels such as coal, oil, and gas for energy. But these fuels cause pollution and one day they will run out. Solar, wind, and water energy will last as long as the Sun shines, the wind blows, and the rivers flow. These renewable energy sources are also "clean," which means they produce very little pollution.

3-second sum-up

We can harness energy from the wind, flowing water, and the Sun.

3-minute mission Compare wind speeds

You need: • Toy pinwheel • Felt-tip pen • Timer

Compare wind speeds with a simple toy pinwheel on a stick. Mark one sail with a felt-tip pen. On a day with light wind, hold the pinwheel into the wind. Use the timer to count how many times the marked sail passes the stick in a minute. Try it another day when you think it's breezier. Were you right?

The power of the Sun, wind, and rain that create our weather are used to produce power.

Wind farm

Solar power plant

Wind farms may have hundreds of turbines.

Hydroelectric power plant

Sunlight lands on layers of special materials that turn it into electricity.

The force of falling water is used to produce power.

Solar panels on roofs turn sunlight into electricity.

Tidal station

The energy from the movement of waves is harnessed to create power.

Climate and seasons

We are all familiar with the changes brought by the seasons, but can you explain exactly why they happen? In many parts of the world, seasonal changes affect the climate—the regular pattern of weather. Experts use weather records over many years to build up a general picture of a region's climate, which includes average temperatures and annual rainfall.

Climate and seasons
Glossary

adapted The way that plants, animals, or people are suited to where they live.

altitude Height above sea level.

Arctic The region of the world around the North Pole.

axis An imaginary line through the center of Earth, around which the planet turns.

biome A large habitat, such as a forest or desert.

conifer A tree with needle-like leaves that produces hard, dry fruit called cones. Most conifers have leaves that stay on the tree all year.

continent One of the large land masses of Earth, such as Europe, Asia, or Africa.

deciduous A tree that loses its leaves each year.

desert An area of land where it rarely rains.

double-glazed Windows with two layers of glass and a space in between, to keep in the heat.

Equator An imaginary horizontal line around the middle of Earth.

evaporate When a liquid changes into a gas without boiling; for example, when a puddle dries up.

evolution The process by which new species (types) of animals and plants develop (evolve) from earlier kinds.

grassland A large area of open land covered with wild grass.

habitat The place where a particular type of animal or plant is normally found.

insulation Material that prevents heat from passing through.

latitude The angular distance of a place, north or south of the Equator.

Northern Hemisphere The half of Earth north of the Equator.

orbit A curved path followed by a planet or an object as it moves around another object in space, such as a sun or planet.

pollution When dirty or harmful substances are added to land, air, or water so that it is no longer safe or pleasant to use.

prey An animal that is hunted, killed, and eaten by another.

rain forest Thick forest in tropical parts of the world that have a lot of rain.

savannah A wide, flat, open area of land, especially in Africa, that is covered with grass and has few trees.

smog A form of air pollution that is or looks like a mixture of smoke and fog, especially in cities.

solar panel A piece of equipment that uses light from the Sun to produce hot water and electricity.

Southern Hemisphere The half of Earth south of the Equator.

temperate Having mild temperatures, which are never very hot or very cold.

tropical Coming from, found in, or typical of the tropics.

tropics The area just above and below the Equator. The climate is warm and hot, and moist all year round.

valley An area of low land between hills or mountains.

Climate

...in 30 seconds

What's the difference between weather and climate?
Weather is whatever is happening in the air at any particular moment—it could be raining or snowing. Climate is the bigger picture—the regular pattern of weather, as measured over many years.

Three main factors affect a region's climate: the distance from the Equator (latitude), the height of the land (altitude), and closeness to the sea.

We've already seen how the Sun heats Earth's surface unevenly, creating three different climate zones—tropical, temperate, and polar. We also know that oceans can affect the climate because they are cooler than the land in summer and warmer in winter, so locations near the sea have cool summers and mild winters. In contrast, places far inland may have extreme conditions, with boiling hot summers and freezing cold winters. This is called a continental climate.

Altitude affects climate too. The higher up you go, the further you are from the warm surface that absorbs the Sun's rays, so it gets colder. To climb Mount Kilimanjaro in tropical Tanzania, you need a sun hat at the base and a wool cap at the top!

3-second sum-up

Climate is the usual pattern of weather in a region.

Seaside weather

Have you been to the beach on vacation? Perhaps you noticed that the weather there is often rainy and windy. That's because moist winds blowing off the ocean shed rain as they hit land and because the difference in temperature between the land and sea produces a strong breeze. This is called a sea breeze.

Climate depends on distance from the Equator, altitude, and distance from the sea.

The snowy peak has a polar climate.

Upper slopes have a cool temperate climate and conifers.

Lower slopes have a warm temperate climate and deciduous trees.

The rain forest has a tropical climate.

Polar region

Temperate zone

Tropical region

Temperate zone

Polar region

Sun's rays

The ocean keeps the coast cool in summer and warm in winter.

Biomes

...in 30 seconds

Different climates suit different plants. Spiky cacti grow well in a desert, but you won't see them in a rain forest. Likewise, rain forest trees such as mahogany would wilt and die in a desert. Varying climates all over Earth create huge habitats called biomes. Each is dominated by a particular type of vegetation, such as grass or conifer trees.

Did you know that nearly a third of Earth's land is covered in trees? Tropical forests grow on either side of the Equator in the warm, wet climate. Woods of broad-leaved trees, such as oaks, grow in temperate regions. A belt of dense, dark conifer forest stretches right across North America, Europe, and Asia. Fir, pine, and spruce trees thrive in this forest belt, called the taiga. Only tiny trees grow north of this in the cold marshy lands of the tundra.

Where the climate is a bit drier, you will find grassland biomes. There are two main types—temperate grasslands and tropical savannah. If there is hardly any rain at all, then deserts form. But some plants such as cacti can survive here since they store moisture in their thick stems. No plants can grow in the polar regions, however, which are permanently covered with ice and snow.

3-second sum-up

Biomes are large regions of Earth with a particular climate and living things.

3-minute mission Which animal lives in which biome?

- polar bear
- jaguar
- zebra
- camel

- desert
- savannah
- polar
- rain forest

Answers on page 93

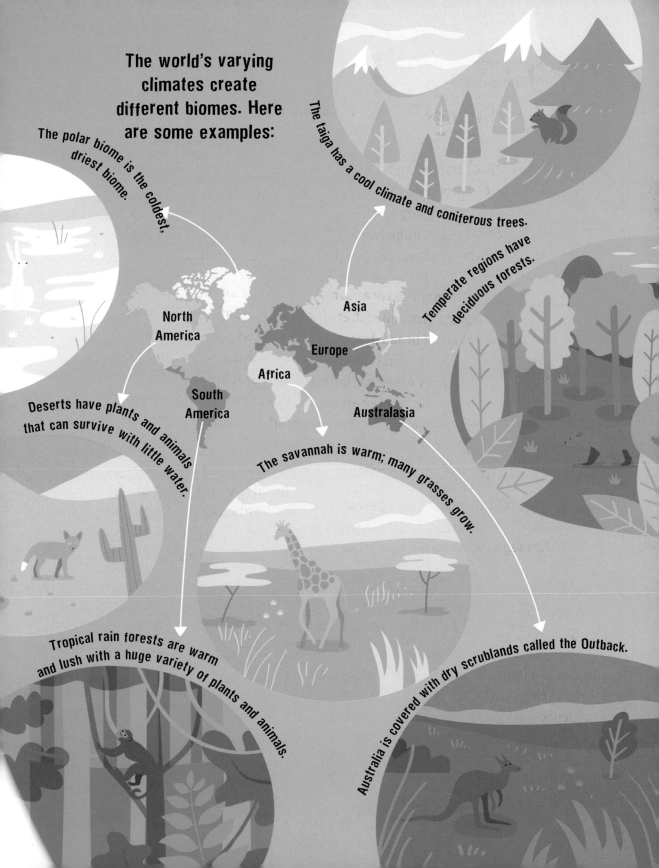

The world's varying climates create different biomes. Here are some examples:

The taiga has a cool climate and coniferous trees.

The polar biome is the coldest, driest biome.

Temperate regions have deciduous forests.

North America

Asia

Europe

Africa

South America

Australasia

Deserts have plants and animals that can survive with little water.

The savannah is warm; many grasses grow.

Tropical rain forests are warm and lush with a huge variety of plants and animals.

Australia is covered with dry scrublands called the Outback.

Microclimates

...in 30 seconds

Biomes can be huge, covering thousands of square miles. Each biome contains many smaller habitats that can have slight differences in climate, such as valleys in mountain regions, or cities surrounded by countryside. These areas are called microclimates.

Have you ever climbed a mountain? Did you notice it getting colder? Mountains are generally cooler as you go up—in fact, the temperature drops 34°F for every 500 feet (150 m) you climb. But because valleys are lower and more sheltered than mountain peaks, they have a warmer microclimate. In steep-sided valleys, villages and towns are often built on the side that gets more sunshine.

Cities are warmer than the surrounding countryside because homes and offices give off heat, which is then trapped, absorbed, and released by the tall buildings. This creates a warm pocket called a heat island. Cities are cozy in winter, but they can be sizzling hot in summer.

City pollution can also affect the local climate. Cars, trucks, factories, and power stations give off fumes, which react with sunlight to form a dirty haze called smog. This can hide the tops of tall buildings and make it hard to breathe.

3-second sum-up

Microclimates are small areas with a different climate than their surroundings.

3-minute mission Height and temperature

The French town of Chamonix lies in a valley in the Alps, close to Mont Blanc, which is 15,800 feet (4,810 m) high. The mountain top can be seen from Chamonix, which lies at 3,400 feet (1,035 m). If the summer daytime temperature in Chamonix is a comfortable 77°F (25°C), what is the temperature at the top of chilly Mont Blanc? **Hint:** Work out the height difference between Chamonix and Mont Blanc and remember how much the temperature drops as you climb.

A village tucked into a mountainside has a warmer microclimate than the nearby mountains.

Some mountain valleys have steep sides.

It is colder in the mountains than at ground level.

Crops grow in the sunshine.

In the shade, the ground is covered in snow.

The village is on the sunny side of the mountain.

The valley bottom is warmer than the slopes above.

Why we have seasons
...in 30 seconds

Seasons happen because Earth tilts on its axis—an imaginary line through the North and South Poles—as it circles the Sun. The tilt is always the same angle in space.

The Equator divides Earth into a top half and a bottom half—the Northern and Southern Hemispheres. When the Southern Hemisphere leans toward the Sun, summer arrives with warm, sunny weather and long daylight hours. In the Northern Hemisphere, it is winter. Earth continues on its orbit and, six months later, the seasons are reversed: the North leans toward the Sun and enjoys summer, while the South has winter.

Tropical regions around the Equator always lean toward the Sun, so it is summer all year around. It sounds ideal—but some parts of the tropics have a dry and a rainy season, so the rainfall is uneven. Temperate regions have four seasons so they have a wide range of weather. Each season lasts for three months.

The polar regions have the most extreme seasons of all. In winter each Pole leans away from the Sun, so it is bitterly cold and completely dark for 24 hours a day. In summer the Pole is bathed in sunlight, and it's light 24/7. Even so, the Sun is low in the sky, so it's still extremely cold.

3-second sum-up

Earth's tilt on its axis produces the seasons.

3-minute mission Show the seasons

You need: • Apple with a stem • Dark room with lamp in the middle

Imagine the stem is the North Pole and the other end the South Pole. Tilt the North Pole toward the lamp (the Sun). It's summer in the Northern Hemisphere. Keeping your apple "Earth" tilted at the same angle in the same direction, move it to the other side of the Sun. Now the Southern Hemisphere has summer!

As Earth orbits the Sun,
the Northern and Southern
Hemispheres have
different seasons.

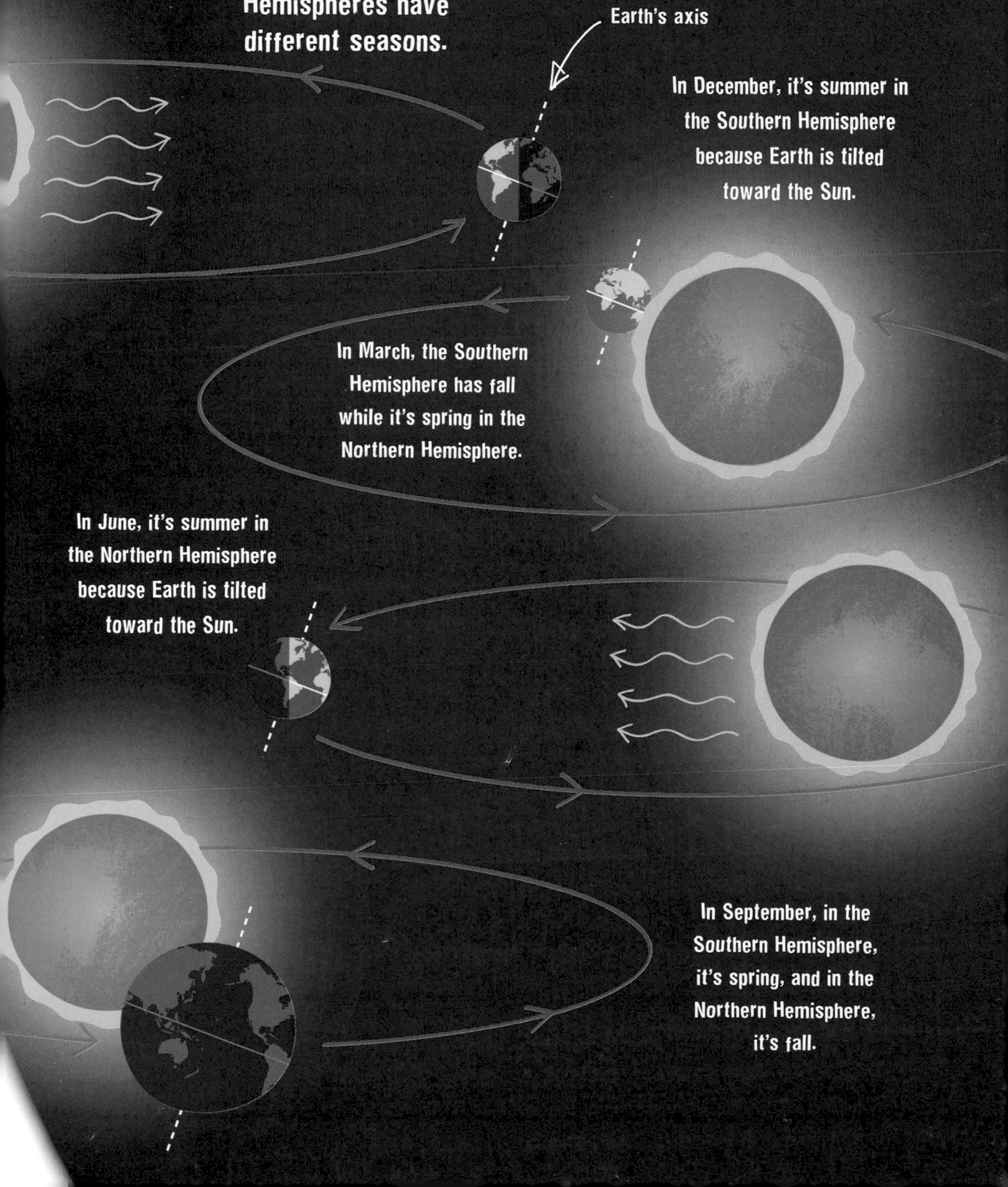

Earth's axis

In December, it's summer in
the Southern Hemisphere
because Earth is tilted
toward the Sun.

In March, the Southern
Hemisphere has fall
while it's spring in the
Northern Hemisphere.

In June, it's summer in
the Northern Hemisphere
because Earth is tilted
toward the Sun.

In September, in the
Southern Hemisphere,
it's spring, and in the
Northern Hemisphere,
it's fall.

Animals in hot and cold lands

...in 30 seconds

Polar bears would badly overheat in the tropics, and tropical animals such as zebras would shiver and shake in the Arctic. All animals are suited to live in a certain climate. Over many generations, different species change to become even better suited to their surroundings. This process is called evolution.

Polar bears, seals, and penguins live in icy cold climates. Most polar animals have a thick coat of fur or feathers to keep out the cold. Underneath is a layer of fat called blubber, which provides insulation. Polar bears and some other animals have a great way to cope with harsh winter weather—they sleep through it! This is called hibernation. But many birds and sea creatures fly or swim to warmer places to avoid the winter chill.

Animals that live in extremely hot places don't have thick coats. Also, their bodies have many other adaptations. For example, desert foxes and rabbits have very large ears that give off heat like radiators and camels can go for days without drinking. Some squirrels even use their tails as sunshades! These animals also stay cool by resting underground or in shady places.

3-second sum-up

Animals have adapted to survive in different climates.

3-minute mission Temperature and evaporation

You need: • 2 towels • Thermometer

Why does washing your face with a wet towel cool you down? Find out on a hot day. Soak one folded towel. Place both towels in the sun for 20 minutes. Then place a thermometer on each folded towel and take the temperature. The difference in temperature is caused by cooling as moisture evaporates from the wet towel.

Polar animals are adapted to life in freezing conditions, while desert animals have evolved to survive in the heat.

Polar bears have thick fur to keep them warm—even on the bottom of their paws.

They have strong legs for walking on snow and swimming through icy water.

Their fur is white so their prey can't spot them.

Polar bears prey on seals and walruses.

Fennec foxes in the African desert have huge ears that lose heat and keep them cool.

The foxes are sand-colored to blend in with the desert so they can hide from prey.

They have fur on the bottom of their feet to protect them from the baking-hot sand.

People in different climates

...in 30 seconds

People have learned to adapt to a variety of climates. We build homes to keep out the cold or let the heat escape, wear suitable clothes for hot or cold weather, and develop technology so we can travel around easily.

Is your home adapted to the climate? If you live in a cold place, your house may have thick walls to provide insulation and double-glazed windows to keep in the heat. If you live in a hot climate, your windows may have shutters to keep the rooms cool and shady when it's hot. In wet climates, floods often occur. Houses are sometimes built on stilts so the flood water doesn't get in. In snowy places, houses have steep roofs so the snow slides off them easily.

Clothes help us to maintain an even body temperature wherever we live. In cold weather, we can wear warm, fleecy tops with hats and scarves. When it's hot, we switch to thin, loose clothing. Lighter or darker colors also help to keep us warm or cool.

To get around in cold, snowy places, people use special snowmobiles—motorized sleds—to drive over ice and snow. In hot places such as a desert, rugged jeeps are needed to navigate the sand.

3-second sum-up

People's clothes, transportation, and homes are adapted to suit the climate they inhabit.

3-minute mission Light and dark colors

You need: • White paper • Dark paper • Thermometer

Place a thermometer in the sun. Cover it with a sheet of white paper. Leave it for half an hour, then check the temperature. Repeat the experiment using a dark piece of paper. From the result of your experiment, what color should you wear to keep cool in the sun?

People survive in various climates by living in different ways.

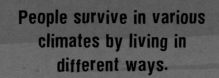

In the Arctic, people wrap up warmly and travel in snowmobiles, which have blades that glide over the ice.

In cold climates, homes have thick walls and double-glazed windows to keep in the heat.

In hot climates, solar panels use energy from the Sun's rays to make electricity.

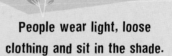

The house has shutters to keep out the heat.

People wear light, loose clothing and sit in the shade.

When there's flooding, people travel by boat.

In wet climates, houses on stilts stay dry during floods.

All kinds of weather

How many types of weather can you name? Earth's weather is incredibly varied. Conditions may be sunny or cloudy, still or windy. Winds bring clouds that may shed rain, hail, sleet, or snow. Frost, fog, and mist may also form. All of these conditions are caused by moisture in the air, which is called humidity.

All kinds of weather
Glossary

air pressure The weight of the air in the atmosphere that presses down toward Earth.

altitude Height above sea level.

condensation The result of a gas changing to a liquid; for example, the drops of water that form on a cold surface when warm water vapor becomes cool.

condense To change from a gas into a liquid; for example, when water vapor turns into water.

continent One of the large land masses of Earth, such as Europe, Asia, or Africa.

current The movement of air or water in a particular direction.

desert An area of land where it rarely rains.

evaporate When a liquid changes into a gas without boiling; for example, when a puddle dries up.

humidity The amount of water vapor in the air.

monsoon A period of heavy rain at a certain time of year due to moist air blowing onto the land.

predict To estimate what will happen in the future. Weather-forecast predictions are produced by supercomputers.

pressure The amount of force that acts over a particular area.

rain forest Thick forest in tropical parts of the world that have a lot of rain.

temperate Having mild temperatures, which are never very hot or very cold.

tropics The area just above and below the Equator. The climate is warm and hot, and moist all year around.

water vapor Water in the form of a gas.

Water cycle

...in 30 seconds

Did you know that moisture moves constantly between land, the air, and the oceans? This is called the water cycle. It means that the water that runs out of your tap was once in the clouds, in the sea, and in rivers or lakes.

As the Sun warms the surface of oceans, lakes, and ponds, moisture evaporates—it rises into the air in the form of a gas called water vapor. The amount of moisture in the air is called humidity. Warm air can hold quite a lot of moisture but when air rises, it cools and the moisture condenses, changing into liquid droplets or ice crystals. These gather to make clouds, which later shed rain or snow.

When it rains, water soaks the ground and is absorbed by plants. But most of it drains away into lakes, ponds, and rivers, which return it to the sea. This completes water's journey and the cycle starts again.

Have you ever looked out of the window and couldn't see a thing? Fog and mist are clouds that form at ground level where warm, moist air condenses as it meets a cold surface such as the ground, the sea, or a lake. When we can see less than 3,300 feet (1 km) through the cloud we call it fog. When we can see between 0.6–1.2 miles (1 and 2 km), it's known as mist.

3-second sum-up

Water goes around and around Earth in the water cycle.

3-minute mission Make a water cycle

You need: • Large bowl • Small glass • Plastic wrap • Pebble

Pour water into the bowl. Put the empty glass in the middle. Cover the bowl tightly with plastic wrap and place the pebble on top. Set the bowl on a sunny windowsill for a few days. Water will appear in the glass! The Sun evaporated the water, which condensed onto the plastic wrap and fell into the bowl—like rain.

Water evaporates into the air as it warms, then condenses and falls back to Earth as it cools.

The clouds shed rain.

The air rises and cools. The moisture condenses and forms clouds.

The Sun's warmth makes water from seas and lakes evaporate into the air.

Most of the rainwater drains into lakes and rivers and returns to the sea.

Some of the rainwater soaks into the ground, where plants absorb it in a process called transpiration.

Clouds

...in 30 seconds

Have you ever wondered how clouds are made? Clouds are floating moisture. They are made of billions of tiny drops of water or ice crystals, which are so light they float on rising air currents.

Clouds form when warm, moist air rises and cools. The water vapor condenses around minute specks of dust to form either water droplets or ice crystals, depending on the temperature. As a gas, water vapor is invisible, but when water droplets or ice crystals clump together they form masses of white or gray clouds.

Look out of the window—can you see any clouds? They can tell you lots about what the weather is going to be like. Clouds form different shapes depending on how high they are, how fast the wind is blowing, and the amount of moisture in the air. Fluffy cumulus clouds look like heaps of cotton wool. If you see these clouds, it will probably be good weather. But when towering, flat-topped cumulonimbus clouds appear, watch out for a thunderstorm!

Cirrus are wispy, high-altitude clouds made of ice crystals. When tufts of cirrus clouds called "mares' tails" dot the sky, storms or rain may be on the way. Stratus clouds cover the sky in a flat gray blanket. These low-altitude clouds may bring rain or snow, or just a dull day. Other cloud types are combinations of cumulus, stratus, and cirrus clouds.

3-second sum-up

Clouds are floating masses of moisture that appear in different forms.

3-minute mission Make a cloud

You need: • Tin can lid • Salt

In a hot and steamy bathroom, put a few grains of salt on the tin can lid. Leave for a few minutes. The grains will turn into droplets as water condenses on the salt—just like in a cloud.

44

Different types of clouds can help you predict what type of weather is coming.

Cirrus means "curl of hair" —just what these clouds look like.

If you see cumulonimbus clouds, a thunderstorm is on its way.

Above 19,700 feet (6,000 m)

6,600–19,700 feet (2,000–6,000 m)

Altocumulus clouds are mid-level clouds.

Up to 6,600 feet (2,000 m)

On fine days, you see cumulus clouds.

Thick gray stratus clouds make the day dull and gray and often mean rain.

Why it rains

...in 30 seconds

All the moisture that collects in clouds will eventually fall as rain, drizzle, sleet, snow, or hail. Any falling moisture, whether in solid form as ice or as liquid water, is known as precipitation.

The tiny water droplets or ice crystals that form clouds are kept up by rising air currents. But as the droplets blow about, they bump into one another and combine to make bigger ones. Finally, they get so big that the air currents cannot support them, so they fall as rain. If snow or hail fall and melt on the way down, they also become rain.

Each raindrop contains about a million water droplets. When you draw raindrops, you probably draw them shaped like teardrops. But small drops are actually round. Big ones are rounded but become flattened as they fall—they have flat tops and bottoms like hamburger buns.

When was the last time you saw a rainbow? A rainbow forms when the Sun shines through falling raindrops. As the light passes through each drop, it is refracted (bent) and splits into a band of colored lights: red, orange, yellow, green, blue, indigo, and violet. Always look in the opposite direction of the Sun to see a rainbow.

3-second sum-up

Rain falls when water droplets get too heavy to float in the air.

3-minute mission Make a rainbow

You need: • Glass of water • Sheet of white paper • Sunny day

Put the glass in the sunshine at the edge of a table, so it is half on, half off—make sure it doesn't fall! Put the paper on the floor so the Sun's rays pass through the water to the paper. Adjust the paper and the glass until you can see a rainbow on the paper.

The droplets of moisture that make up a raincloud fall as rain.

Ice crystals usually melt and form raindrops, but if it's really cold near the ground, they fall as snow.

At the top of the cloud are ice crystals.

Water droplet

Ice crystal

Raindrop shapes

⅛ inch ¼ inch ½ inch

At the bottom of the cloud are water drops only. They combine to form raindrops.

A rainbow forms as sunlight enters raindrops and is reflected out again.

When the air can no longer support the raindrops, they fall as rain.

Rainfall patterns

...in 30 seconds

Rain is vital to plants and animals on land. People need it for drinking, farming, and industry. However, rain does not fall in equal amounts over Earth. Some places have high rainfall and flooding, while others are so dry there is little rain from one year to the next.

In the tropics, land near the coast has a lot of rain because warm, moist air moves in from the oceans. Dense rain forests grow in these wet conditions. Near the center of continents, far away from moist ocean winds, there may be deserts where little grows.

Did you know that the polar regions can be described as deserts, too? There's plenty of water, but it's all locked up as ice, so clouds do not form and barely any rain falls.

Sometimes you find places with high rainfall just a few miles from a very dry spot. This can happen in mountain ranges. Moist air blowing off the ocean rises and cools as it reaches the mountain to form clouds that shed all their rain on the side facing the sea. By the time the cloud reaches the other side, it has no moisture left. The resulting dry area is called a rain shadow.

3-second sum-up

Some places get a lot of rain while others get very little.

Monsoon climate

In a temperate climate, there are rainy and sunny days throughout the year. It's different in parts of the tropics that have a monsoon climate. These places have a dry season and a rainy season, and the weather goes from one extreme to another. India lies in the path of monsoon winds. In summer, moist winds blowing off the ocean bring torrential rain. In winter, dry wind blows from the opposite direction, across Central Asia, so hardly any rain falls.

Snow, sleet, hail, and frost

...in 30 seconds

High in the air, temperatures fall below zero. It's cold enough for snow! Snowflakes form when moisture freezes into ice crystals in clouds. As ice crystals bump together they combine and get bigger. Eventually, they grow so heavy they fall to the ground. If the ground temperature is just above zero, the flakes partly melt. These partly melted flakes are called sleet.

Snowflakes usually contain more than 100 crystals, arranged in a structure called a lattice. All snowflakes have six points and no two snowflakes are the same.

Hail forms when pellets of ice are tossed up and down inside storm clouds. Each time the pellet rises and falls it receives a fresh coating of ice. Near the cloud top, frosty layers are added as moisture freezes quickly.

Frost is ice that forms at ground level when moisture condenses and freezes on cold surfaces such as glass or leaves. Beautiful, feathery patterns form on window panes as ice crystals grow outward. When fog blankets the landscape, the water droplets in the fog can freeze onto branches and twigs to create a thick frost called rime.

3-second sum-up

Snow, hail, frost, and sleet are all forms of ice.

Champion hail

Most hailstones are the size of peas, but some can be as big as tennis balls, and the largest are the size of grapefruits! The largest hailstone ever recorded fell in South Dakota in 2010. It was 8 inches (20 cm) across and weighed 1.94 pounds (0.88 kg). You wouldn't want to be in the way when a whopper like this crashed to the ground!

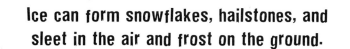

Ice can form snowflakes, hailstones, and
sleet in the air and frost on the ground.

Snowflakes

Snowflakes are made of
single ice crystals that grow
in hexagonal patterns.

Hailstones

Hailstones are made of layers of
frozen water. You can see the layers
if you cut a hailstone in two. For
large hailstones to stay in the air
while they are growing, air has to be
rising rapidly in the thunderclouds.

Sleet

If snowflakes pass through
a layer of warmer air, they
partly melt to form sleet.

Frost forms at ground
level, especially on clear
winter nights.

Highs, lows, and fronts

...in 30 seconds

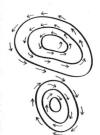

Rising and sinking air produces areas with different air pressure. When air rises, it creates an area of low pressure below it, known as a "low." The air around this area swirls around. If it does not swirl fast enough—for example, because of friction with the surface—it is drawn inward and upward. As the moist air rises to where the air pressure is lower, it expands and cools, producing clouds and rain. This unsettled weather can last for days.

Where air sinks, it creates a "high"—a zone of high pressure. The sinking air is squashed and warm, preventing condensation from forming rainclouds. So highs often bring settled conditions with fine, sunny weather.

Weather forecasts often mention weather fronts. These are sloping boundaries between warm and cold air masses. They are named after the temperature of the air that is moving forward. In a warm front, a mass of warm air slowly slides above cold air. As warm air rises, it expands and cools so that moisture condenses, bringing clouds and drizzle. Cold fronts can produce dramatic weather. In a cold front, a mass of cold air burrows under warm air, making it rise quickly. Moisture condenses rapidly and can cause thunderstorms and heavy rain.

3-second sum-up

Different air pressure and temperature cause different types of weather.

3-minute mission Make a "low"

You need: • Half cup of tea made with tea leaves • Teaspoon

The air surrounding highs and lows spirals around like water swirling around a drain. You can create a similar effect using a cup of tea with tea leaves at the bottom. Stir the tea with a spoon. The tea leaves that collect at the center are like air moving inward and upward in a low pressure system.

A warm weather front brings
clouds and drizzle while a
cold weather front may
bring thunderstorms.

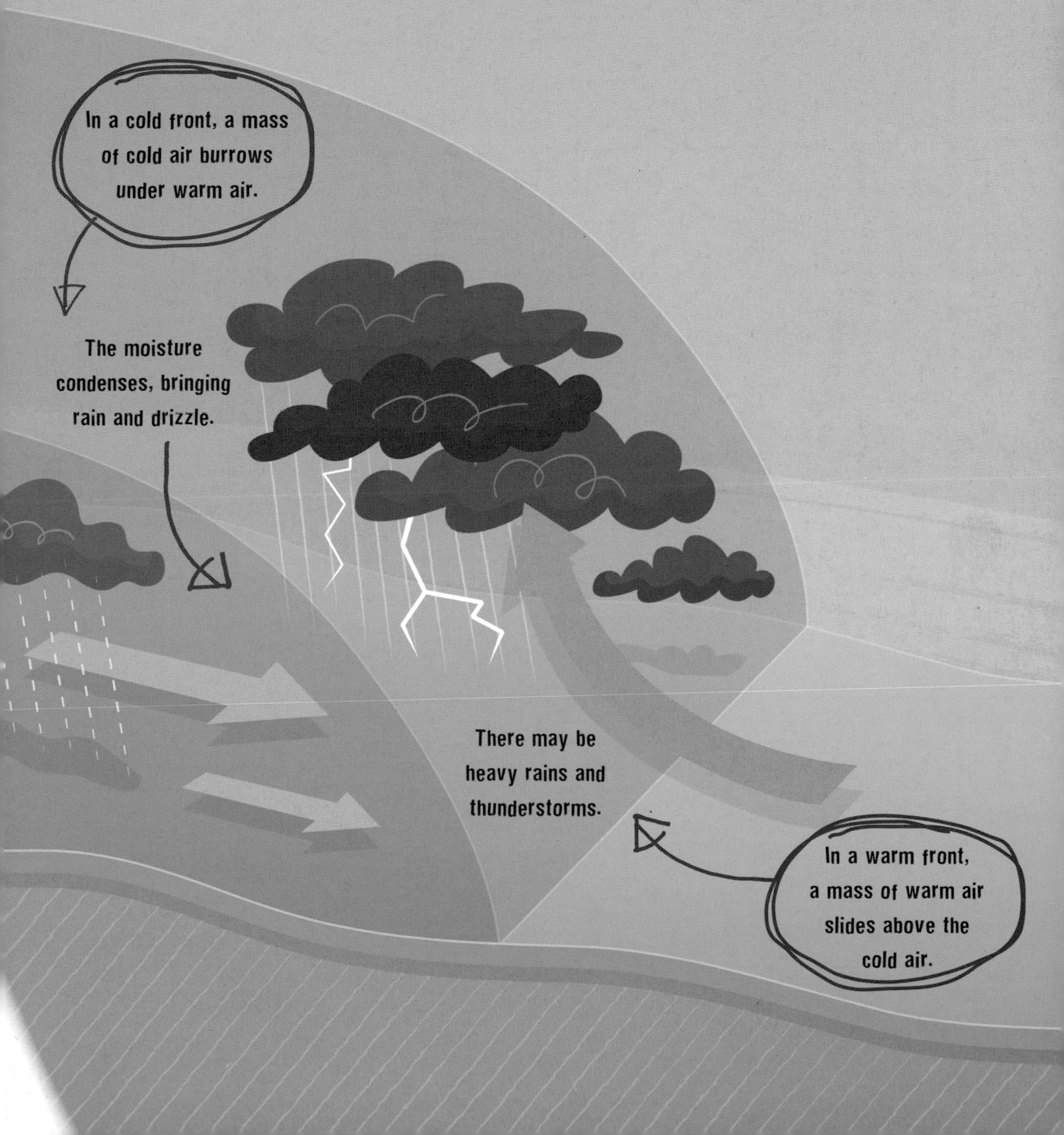

In a cold front, a mass
of cold air burrows
under warm air.

The moisture
condenses, bringing
rain and drizzle.

There may be
heavy rains and
thunderstorms.

In a warm front,
a mass of warm air
slides above the
cold air.

Extreme weather

The weather can seem gentle on a mild and sunny day. But it can also turn nasty. Extreme weather includes thunderstorms, blizzards, hailstorms, hurricanes, and tornadoes. These severe weather systems can sometimes be quite destructive. This chapter explores the chaos that results when dangerous weather hits the planet.

Extreme weather
Glossary

centrifugal force The outward force on an object traveling in a circle.

cloudburst A sudden heavy fall of rain.

condensation The process of a gas changing to a liquid; for example, the drops of water that form on a cold surface when warm water vapor becomes cool.

condense To change from a gas into a liquid; for example, when water vapor turns into water.

current The movement of air or water in a particular direction.

cyclone A weather system with low pressure in the middle and strong winds swirling around.

desert An area of land where it rarely rains.

Equator An imaginary horizontal line around the middle of Earth.

fertile Of land or soil, where plants grow well.

friction The resistance (the force that stops something moving) of one surface sliding against another surface.

hurricane A violent storm with very strong winds, found especially over the western Atlantic Ocean.

landslide A mass of earth or rock that falls down the slope of a mountain or a cliff.

monsoon A period of heavy rain at a certain time of year due to moist air blowing onto the land.

predict To try to estimate what will happen in the future. Weather-forecast predictions are produced by supercomputers.

pressure The amount of force that acts over a particular area.

repel When two things repel each other, an electrical or magnetic force pushes them apart.

snowdrift A deep pile of snow that has been blown together by the wind.

tide The regular rise and fall in the level of the sea, caused by the pull of the Moon and the rotation of Earth.

tropical Coming from, found in, or typical of the tropics.

typhoon A weather system with low pressure in the middle and strong winds swirling around.

valley An area of low land between hills or mountains.

Thunderstorms

...in 30 seconds

Every year about 16 million thunderstorms strike somewhere on Earth—that's an average of 45,000 every day! Thunderstorms are the most common form of extreme weather. How do they happen?

Inside towering thunderclouds, powerful air currents cause water droplets, hail, and ice crystals to rub together. The resulting friction produces static electricity. The top of the cloud develops a positive charge while the bottom becomes negatively charged. The ground below the cloud also becomes positively charged.

When the charge is great enough, a powerful electric spark leaps inside the cloud, between clouds, or from the cloud to the ground. That's when you see a flash of lightning. As lightning streaks through the air, it superheats it, making the air expand rapidly. This sets up a shock wave, and boom! We hear thunder.

Lighting and thunder happen at the same time, but you see the lightning first. This is because light travels faster than sound. You can count the number of seconds between the lightning flash and the thunder to figure out the distance of the storm. Light reaches you almost instantly while sound takes 5 seconds to cover 1 mile (3 seconds to travel 1 km). So 15 seconds between lightning and thunder means the storm is 3 miles (5 km) away.

3-second sum-up

Thunderstorms are caused by powerful electric charges inside clouds.

3-minute mission Make static electricity

You need: • Inflated balloon • Very thin plastic bag • Dish towel

Cut a 1-inch (2.5-cm) strip from the middle of the bag to make a loop. Put the loop on a table and stroke it with the dish towel. Rub the balloon on your hair. Toss the loop into the air. Put the charged balloon underneath it—the loop will float above it! The loop and balloon are electrically charged and repel each other.

Thunder and lightning happen
when an electric charge
builds up inside a cloud.

A positive charge
develops at the top of
the cloud.

A negative charge
develops at the
bottom of the cloud.

Lightning can also leap
from cloud to cloud.

A positive charge develops
on the ground below.

A powerful electric spark
leaps from the cloud to
the ground—lightning!

Hurricanes

...in 30 seconds

A hurricane is an enormous spinning storm up to 600 miles (1,000 km) wide. From space, it looks like a giant pinwheel of cloud speeding across Earth's surface. Hurricanes are some of the most destructive forces in nature.

Called hurricanes in the Atlantic Ocean, in the Pacific Ocean they are called typhoons, and in the Indian Ocean, cyclones.

Hurricanes form over tropical oceans in summer and fall where the sea is warm and the air moist. They begin as a cluster of thunderstorms. Warm air rises rapidly and causes low pressure. The storm spins faster around this low pressure as more air rises and water condenses as heavy rain, releasing heat and fueling the storm further.

Inside the hurricane, there is a calm center called the eye. But around this the most powerful winds swirl at up to 185 miles per hour (300 km per hour) —as fast as the highest-speed trains.

Especially when it hits hard, a hurricane's whirling winds and torrential rain can cause destruction. Winds circling the eye produce an area of very low pressure, which can suck up water from the sea to form a storm surge. When this surge reaches the land, it rises up like a high tide and smashes into the coast.

3-second sum-up

Hurricanes are the most powerful storms on Earth.

Wrecked by a storm surge

In 2013, Typhoon Haiyan tore through the central Philippines, bringing torrential rains, ferocious winds of over 170 miles per hour (270 km per hour), and a storm surge of over 25 feet (7.5 m). It devastated coastal areas, killing 6,000 people and damaging or destroying the homes of 4 million people.

A hurricane forms over the ocean and slams into the land, causing great damage.

Hurricanes begin as thunderstorms over tropical oceans.

Heavy rain falls. It releases heat and fuels the storm.

Air expands and cools as it rises, causing condensation and clouds to form.

Light winds around the hurricane allow it to grow.

Warm air rises rapidly upward.

Winds swirl around the eye of the hurricane.

When the hurricane approaches land, the winds create an area of low pressure and suck up a mass of water called a storm surge.

The storm floods the land and the hurricane's winds destroy buildings and trees.

Tornadoes

...in 30 seconds

A tornado is a violent spinning storm. In contrast to hurricanes, they are tiny—just a half mile (1 km) or so across—and last only a few minutes, while hurricanes blow for days. Yet the winds inside a tornado are even more ferocious than those of a hurricane. Whirling at up to 300 miles per hour (480 km per hour), they're the fastest winds on Earth.

Tornadoes form on land, below powerful thunderstorms called supercells. Warm air rushing upward starts to spiral. A spinning funnel of air called a vortex appears below the cloud and reaches down like an elephant's trunk. When it hits the ground, it becomes a tornado.

The whirling air exerts a tremendous sucking force, like a giant vacuum cleaner. Crops and trees are uprooted. Cars, trucks, boats, and sheds are pulled into the air and hurled around like toys. Roofs are wrenched off houses. As a tornado weaves through the landscape, it leaves a narrow trail of total destruction.

Sometimes whole groups of tornadoes strike at once. This is called a swarm, and it most often happens in the south-central United States, in a storm-prone area called Tornado Alley. In 1974 a swarm of 148 tornadoes hit this region, leaving a trail of destruction 2,500 miles (4,000 km) long.

3-second sum-up

Tornadoes are whirling columns of air with destructively strong winds.

3-minute mission Tornado protection

Tornadoes are incredibly powerful and can destroy entire neighborhoods. Think about your own home. Would it survive a fierce storm? Imagine that you are an architect in a country that is prone to tornadoes. Think of ways to protect homes from strong winds. Then go online to find out how architects design such buildings. Are there any similarities to your ideas?

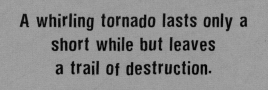

A whirling tornado lasts only a short while but leaves a trail of destruction.

Winds spiraling around a center of low pressure exert centrifugal force, pushing outward like the force you feel on a merry-go-round.

Tornadoes form below thunderclouds when winds start to spiral upward.

A dark funnel of air forms below the clouds.

This center of very low pressure exerts a sucking force.

The tornado leaves a trail of destruction in its wake.

Deserts and droughts

...in 30 seconds

Picture a desert. The chances are you think of a hot, sandy place. Deserts such as the Sahara are indeed scorching hot by day—but they are extremely cold at night because there are no clouds to keep in the heat. Some deserts are bitterly cold by day, too. In fact, most deserts are rocky or stony—not sandy at all.

All deserts are ultra-dry places that receive less than 10 inches (25 cm) of rain a year. Many of the world's great deserts are found in two bands lying between 15° and 30° north or south of the Equator. In these areas, warm, dry air sinks, which prevents rain clouds from forming.

Ultra-dry conditions are normal in deserts, but droughts are a lot less predictable. A drought is an unusually long period of dry weather that can devastate places that are usually fertile. Rivers and lakes dry up, crops wither, and animals die of thirst. The parched conditions can spark forest fires. People may have to leave or face starvation.

In the 1930s the American Midwest suffered one of the most famous droughts in history. Years of dry weather turned the earth to dust, then high winds blew it away, filling the air with the choking dust. Farming families were forced to flee and it took years to restore the land.

3-second sum-up

Deserts are ultra-dry places. Droughts are unusually dry weather.

Droughts down under

Australia has had some of the worst droughts on record, with disastrous effects on farming. In cities, people learned to reuse "gray water"—waste water that had been used in showers, baths, and sinks. Water treatment plants filtered the salt out of sea water, making it safe to drink. Other people in dry places can learn this lesson too. They can save water by reusing gray water for watering plants or washing the car.

When a drought strikes, it brings desert-like conditions, devastating farmland and killing crops and livestock.

Forest fires start in ultra-dry conditions.

Water supplies run out.

Barns are empty of grain and farm machinery stands idle.

Trees and crops die from lack of water.

The soil is cracked and dry.

Floods

...in 30 seconds

Parts of the world are ultra-dry; others have the opposite problem —they are prone to flooding from rivers, the oceans, and flash floods.

There are two main types of flooding: river and coastal floods. River floods occur after heavy rain, especially in tropical regions where there is a rainy season known as a monsoon. The rivers may burst their banks, gushing over the surrounding land. In 2011 Southeast Asia was hit by ultra-heavy monsoon rains. Destructive floods swept through Thailand, Vietnam, and Cambodia, and 1,800 people died.

Coastal floods may be caused by high tides, huge storms, hurricanes, or tsunamis—giant waves set off by earthquakes.

Flash floods are sudden floods that strike in narrow mountain valleys. Violent downpours called cloudbursts send a wall of water surging down, sweeping away roads, bridges, cars, and houses. In 2004 one month's rain fell in just two hours in a narrow valley in Cornwall, England, creating a flash flood. It engulfed the village of Boscastle, causing extensive damage.

Even in deserts, cloudbursts can trigger flash floods. The stony ground is too dry to absorb the rapidly falling rain, which streams off the land. The water gushes into valleys and stream beds, which overflow into the desert.

3-second sum-up

Floods mainly affect river valleys and coasts.

Days of downpours

In June 2013 North India suffered ultra-heavy rains. Cloudbursts usually only last minutes, but these downpours lasted for four days. The torrential rain triggered floods and devastating landslides. Bridges and entire villages were swept away.

Torrential rain in a narrow
mountain valley can cause flash
flooding and serious damage
to people's homes.

A cloudburst in
the mountains far
upstream causes a
flash flood.

People may
climb onto the roofs of
houses to avoid being
swept away.

A wall of water builds
up as many streams
combine.

The river bursts its banks.

The emergency services
rescue people by boat.

Trees and cars can be
swept away by the
muddy torrent
of water.

Blizzards and hailstorms

...in 30 seconds

Have you ever been caught in a blizzard, hailstorm, or ice storm? Blizzards are severe snowstorms with howling winds. The air is filled with stinging snow, so you can't see anything—it's a whiteout! In 2010, record blizzards struck the eastern United States. Cities were buried in up to 30 inches (75 cm) of snow. Many people were stranded as buses, trains, and subways stopped running and airports closed.

Heavy snow can cause mayhem, snapping trees in half, bringing power lines crashing down and cutting off electricity. When thick snow blocks the roads, homes can be isolated for days and cars can get stuck in snowdrifts.

In steep mountain areas, heavy snowfall can trigger an avalanche. A large mass of snow suddenly breaks away from the mountain and hurtles downhill, sweeping away trees, houses, and people.

Violent hailstorms can be dangerous, too. Hailstones the size of golf balls can shatter glass roofs, skylights, and car windshields. In May 1995, the town of Forth Worth, Texas, was hit by a hailstorm that caused $2 billion in damages. Fourteen people died.

Ice storms are quite common in North America. Freezing rain falls, coating roads, houses, and power lines in a thick glaze of ice that can damage buildings and cause traffic accidents.

3-second sum-up

Severe winter weather can put lives at risk.

Ice meteors

Huge dangerous chunks of ice called ice meteors occasionally fall from the sky. They probably come from aircraft. In 2007, a 20-pound (9-kg) lump of ice—that's the weight of nine bags of sugar—crashed through the roof of a warehouse in Spain. The massive chunk fell out of a clear sky.

Villages, towns, and even cities can be buried by snow during a blizzard.

Strong winds and snow

A mass of snow, ice, and rocks may fall rapidly down the mountainside in an avalanche.

If power lines are damaged, electricity to homes is cut off.

Snow and ice can block roads. The snowdrifts can bury cars.

Trees snap under the weight of snow.

Predicting the weather

We all want to know what the weather will be like tomorrow and we rely on weather forecasts to tell us. Weather science is not new, but in the last 30 years or so, the methods we use to measure the weather have become a lot more sophisticated. Experts are now much better at predicting the weather with computer models based on science, but the weather still holds surprises!

Predicting the weather
Glossary

air pressure The weight of the air in the atmosphere that presses down toward Earth.

atmosphere The mixture of gases that surrounds Earth.

buoy An object that floats on the sea or a river to mark areas where it is dangerous and where it is safe for boats to go. Weather stations can be placed on buoys.

current The movement of air or water in a particular direction.

cyclone A weather system with low pressure in the middle and strong winds swirling around.

humidity The amount of water vapor in the air.

hurricane A violent storm with strong winds, especially over the western Atlantic Ocean.

infrared Heat radiation or waves that are longer than those of red light in the color spectrum, and which cannot be seen.

meteorologist A scientist who studies and forecasts Earth's atmosphere and its changes.

orbit A curved path followed by a planet or an object as it moves around another object in space, such as a sun or planet.

predict To try to estimate what will happen in the future. Weather-forecast predictions are produced by supercomputers.

pressure The amount of force that acts over a particular area.

radar A system that uses radio waves to find the position and movement of objects. It can be used to measure weather conditions.

satellite An electronic device that is sent into space to orbit Earth or another planet. It can be used for collecting weather data.

smog A form of air pollution that is or looks like a mixture of smoke and fog, especially in cities.

solar panel A piece of equipment that uses light from the Sun to produce hot water and electricity.

wildfire An uncontrolled fire that burns everything in its path.

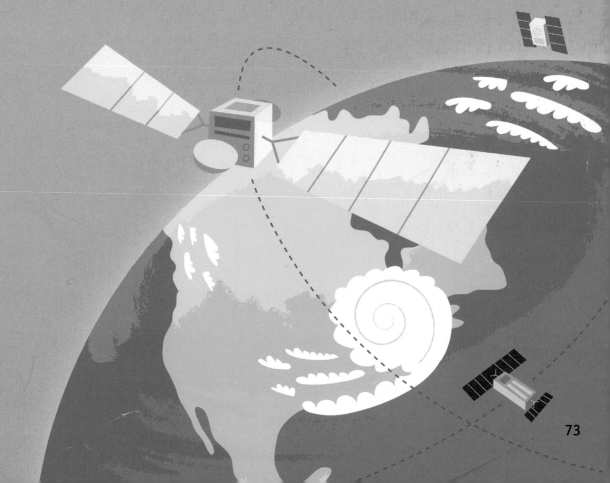

Studying the weather

...in 30 seconds

Meteorology is the scientific study of the weather, and the men and women who study the atmosphere are called meteorologists. People have been studying the weather for years, but high-tech equipment now allows us to produce far more accurate forecasts.

Some weather conditions are still measured traditionally, using instruments such as thermometers to record temperature and barometers to show air pressure. Anemometers have little cups that spin in the wind to record wind speeds, while rain gauges record rainfall and snowfall.

Weather conditions are monitored by thousands of weather stations on land, on ships, and on buoys at sea. Up in the air, weather planes equipped with radar and hydrogen-filled balloons measure clouds and conditions high in the atmosphere.

Today, we can feed all this information into supercomputers, which can produce a more accurate forecast than traditional instruments alone. Short-term forecasts for the next day or so are usually pretty accurate, but it's still very difficult to say what the weather will be like over several weeks.

3-second sum-up

Scientists use many different instruments to study the weather.

3-minute mission Make a rain gauge

You need: • Plastic bottle • Scissors • Ruler • Adhesive tape

You can be a meteorologist, too! Cut the bottle in half. Put the top upside-down in the base to make a funnel. Tape a ruler to the side to measure the rain. Place your rain gauge on the ground outside. Check and empty it once a day and record the total rainfall for a week.

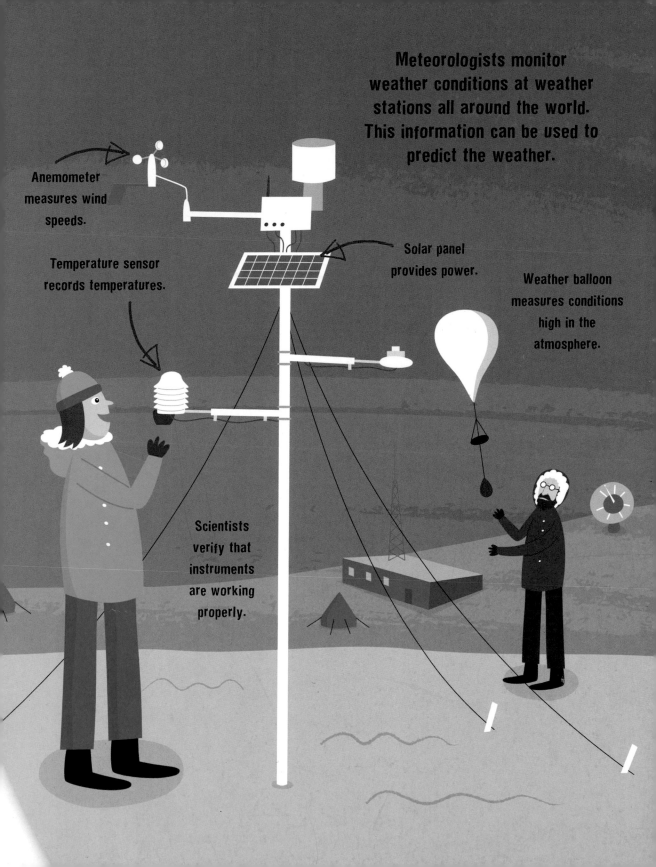

Meteorologists monitor weather conditions at weather stations all around the world. This information can be used to predict the weather.

Anemometer measures wind speeds.

Temperature sensor records temperatures.

Solar panel provides power.

Weather balloon measures conditions high in the atmosphere.

Scientists verify that instruments are working properly.

Satellites

...in 30 seconds

How do weather forecasters know it's going to rain?
Meteorologists use satellites orbiting high above Earth to collect weather data. The satellites have cameras that can photograph clouds and track storms and hurricanes. This helps scientists figure out where storms will strike, so local people can be warned. Some satellites have infrared cameras that detect heat in order to record temperatures and humidity.

Weather satellites also monitor city smog, smoke from forest fires, and ash from volcanoes, as well as track ocean currents. These "eyes in the sky" normally operate automatically, but they can also be controlled from the ground.

The first weather satellite, TIROS-1, was shot into space on a rocket on April 1st 1960. It was mostly designed for TV broadcasting, but also carried infrared instruments for weather measurements. Over the next few decades, this technology transformed weather forecasts. Satellites could collect weather data from across the planet, including the most remote places.

There are two main weather satellites. Geostationary satellites orbit at heights of approximately 22,300 miles (36,000 km). They complete one orbit every 24 hours with Earth's rotation. Polar orbiting satellites take one to two hours to circle Earth at a height of approximately 530 miles (850 km).

3-second sum-up

Weather satellites record clouds, storms, temperature, and humidity.

3-minute mission Live satellite images

Pick a country in a different part of the world. Go online and search for live weather satellite pictures, plus the name of your chosen country. Take a look at the weather. How is it different? Are there any similarities? How would your life be different if you lived in that climate?

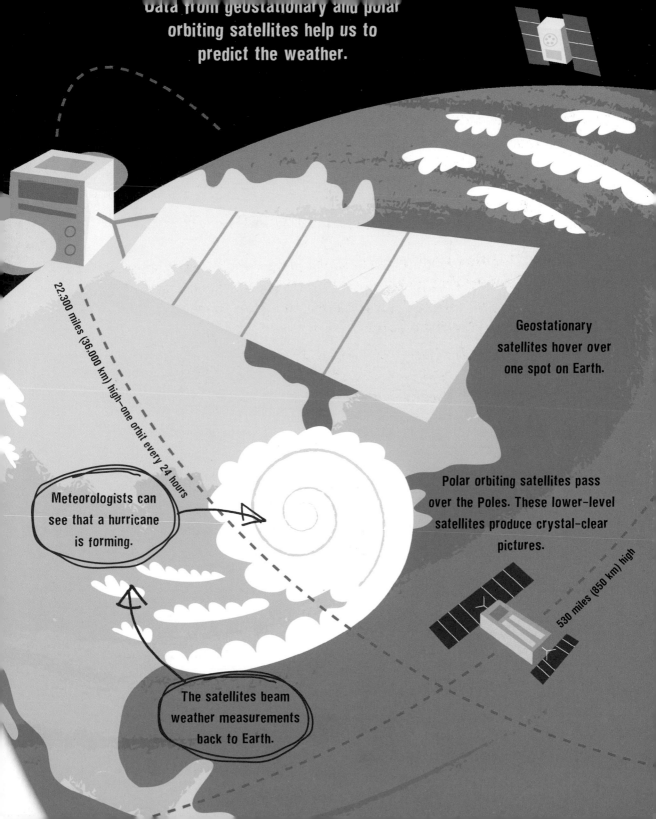

Data from geostationary and polar orbiting satellites help us to predict the weather.

Geostationary satellites hover over one spot on Earth.

Polar orbiting satellites pass over the Poles. These lower-level satellites produce crystal-clear pictures.

22,300 miles (36,000 km) high—one orbit every 24 hours

530 miles (850 km) high

Meteorologists can see that a hurricane is forming.

The satellites beam weather measurements back to Earth.

Forecasts and weather maps

...in 30 seconds

Will you need sunglasses or a raincoat tomorrow? If you've seen the weather forecast, you will know the answer!

Weather forecasts help us plan our day. They are especially useful for people who work outdoors, such as farmers, construction workers, and coast guards, and for airline, train, and ferry companies. Weather forecasts help to keep us safe. If severe weather such as snow, hail, or a flood is expected, scientists issue warnings and recommend precautions.

Weather forecasts are shown on maps called synoptic charts. Synoptic means "seen together." This is because the charts are made using data taken from many different places at the same time.

Variations in air pressure affect the weather, so air pressure is one of the main things shown on weather maps. Lines called isobars link areas of equal air pressure. Isobars form rings around lows (low pressure zones) and highs (high pressure zones), which are associated with certain kinds of weather (see page 52).

Using different symbols, weather maps show warm fronts and cold fronts —bands of advancing warm or cold air that may bring clouds and rain. They also show wind speeds and directions. Now when you see a weather map on TV, you'll understand what it means!

3-second sum-up

Weather forecasts are useful to help people plan ahead.

3-minute mission Pinecone predictions

In days gone by, people used natural objects such as pinecones to predict the weather. In dry weather, pinecones' scales open up. In damp conditions, the scales absorb moisture and close up—a sign that rain is on the way. Test it out for yourself—can a pinecone predict the weather?

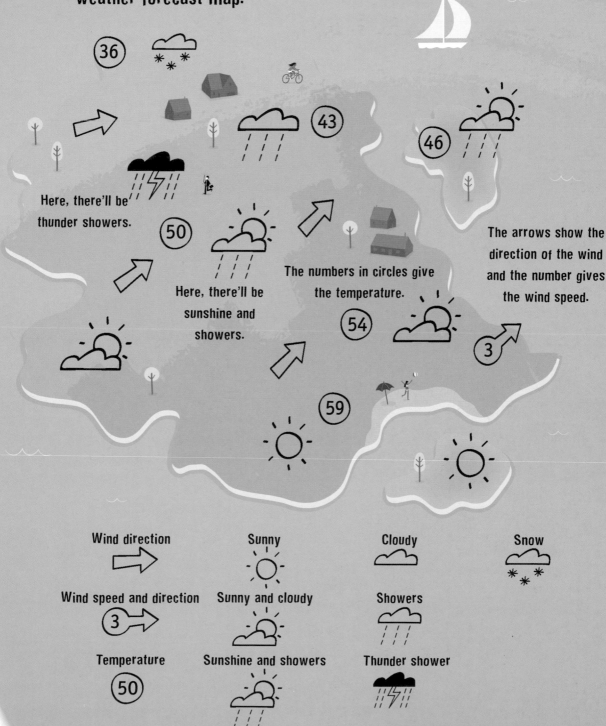

Data about the weather is collected and fed into computers, which make predictions that are presented as a weather forecast map.

Here, there'll be thunder showers.

Here, there'll be sunshine and showers.

The numbers in circles give the temperature.

The arrows show the direction of the wind and the number gives the wind speed.

Wind direction

Sunny

Cloudy

Snow

Wind speed and direction

Sunny and cloudy

Showers

Temperature

Sunshine and showers

Thunder shower

Mysterious weather

...in 30 seconds

Extreme weather events such as hurricanes unleash incredible energy. It's not surprising that in ancient times, people thought gods were responsible for scary weather. The Romans believed that the god Jupiter hurled thunderbolts and caused thunderstorms. In dry regions, people worshipped rain gods and performed special ceremonies, pleading with the gods to send rain.

Today, we understand much more about the weather, but some rare events are still hard to explain. Weird and wonderful kinds of weather include sting jets, which form on intense cyclones. The "sting in the tail" of the cyclone brings fierce winds. In thunderstorms, ship masts and aircraft wings sometimes give off an eerie glow called St. Elmo's fire—the light comes from a discharge of electricity.

Throughout history, people have reported showers of fish, frogs, spiders, jellyfish, and worms raining down from the sky. Experts believe these strange showers are caused by powerful currents of rising air that pluck animals from the sea or land and drop them down in another place.

Other weird events include orange or purple snow, shining clouds, and microbursts, which are sudden, powerful downblasts of air that can sweep an aircraft out of the sky and cause a fatal crash.

3-second sum-up

Some rare weather events are still a mystery.

Fire whirls

A fire whirl is a tornado of fire, often caused by a tornado spinning close to a wildfire. The fire becomes part of the storm, creating a fierce whirlwind of flames that burns for a few minutes. Fire whirls are rare, but when they do occur, the combination of raging fire and fast winds can be devastating.

We still don't understand such rare weather events as sting jets, microbursts, showers of frogs, or St. Elmo's fire.

An aircraft may give off a glow during a thunderstorm, called St. Elmo's fire.

The sting jet brings fierce swirling winds raging at more than 100 mph (160 kph).

A microburst is a sudden downward blast of air.

A shower of frogs rains on the land.

Climate change

Climate and weather are always in the news these days. That is because scientists have discovered that Earth's climate is getting warmer—this is called global warming. Climate change happens naturally, but usually quite slowly. Now human activities are changing the balance of gases in the air, which is causing more rapid change. This chapter explores how and why climate change is happening, and how it could affect us.

Climate change
Glossary

Antarctica The region of the world around the South Pole.

Arctic The region of the world around the North Pole.

atmosphere The mixture of gases that surrounds Earth.

axis An imaginary horizontal line through the center of Earth, around which it turns.

emit To send out something, such as light or heat.

fossil fuel A fuel, such as coal or oil, that was formed over millions of years from the remains of animals or plants.

glacier A large mass of ice, formed by snow on mountains, that moves, very slowly, down a valley.

global warming Rising temperatures worldwide, caused by the increase of particular gases, especially carbon dioxide, in the atmosphere. Some of these gases are produced by human activity.

hurricane A violent storm with strong winds, especially over the western Atlantic Ocean.

hydroelectric power Using the power of water to produce electricity.

ice age One of the long periods of time, thousands of years ago, when Earth's climate was cooler and much of its surface was covered in ice.

orbit A curved path followed by a planet or an object as it moves around another object in space, such as a sun or planet.

pollution When dirty or harmful substances are added to land, air, or water so that it is no longer safe or pleasant to use.

solar power Turning energy from the Sun's rays into energy that people can use.

water vapor Water in the form of a gas.

Climate change

...in 30 seconds

People often ask if climate change is normal. Earth's climate changes naturally and slowly over time. During the ice ages, temperatures were far colder—during the last one, ice covered about 30 percent of Earth's surface. Much of Europe, Asia, and North America was frozen wasteland, buried in great ice sheets called glaciers.

Over the last 2 million years, there have been at least 15 ice ages. In between there were warmer periods called interglacials. But Earth's climate has been slowly and steadily warming since the last ice age ended 10,000 years ago.

Climate change happens naturally because Earth wobbles on its axis as it circles the Sun, and Earth's tilt on its axis also alters slightly. Earth's orbit is not completely round either. These natural climate changes happen extremely slowly.

Volcanic eruptions can also affect the climate. In 1815, Mount Tambora in Indonesia erupted violently, shooting gases, dust, and rocks high into the atmosphere, where they spread out and blocked sunlight. Parts of the planet were chilled for many months, causing crop failure and hunger.

But now Earth's climate is changing faster than ever because of air pollution caused by people.

3-second sum-up

Earth's climate changes naturally, but only very slowly.

Animals and climate change

Climate change affects animals as well as humans. In the polar regions, the melting ice caps are disastrous for wildlife. Polar bears rely on sea ice (frozen seawater on the ocean's surface) for hunting their seal prey, so it's becoming harder for them to feed and for their cubs to survive. Emperor penguins in Antarctica also depend on sea ice for breeding and raising their chicks.

In the past, only natural factors affected Earth's climate, causing gradual changes over time. In today's polluted world, the rate of change is speeding up.

Last ice age:
30% ice coverage

More recent times:
10% ice coverage

Ice covered large areas during the last Ice Age.

As the ice age ended, the climate warmed and many glaciers melted.

Sea levels rose as melted ice drained into the oceans.

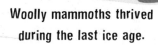

Woolly mammoths thrived during the last ice age.

Global warming

...in 30 seconds

Earth's atmosphere helps to keep conditions comfortable and warm so life can flourish. Carbon dioxide and water vapor in the air allow sunlight through to warm our planet and prevent some of the heat emitted from Earth's surface from escaping into space.

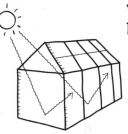

These gases act a bit like the glass in a greenhouse that keeps our plants warm—we call them "greenhouse gases." This natural warming is called the Greenhouse Effect. Without it, Earth would be about 91°F colder than it is today—far too cold for life to exist.

In the last 150 years or so, people have been adding more greenhouse gases to the atmosphere. As power stations, factories, cars, and homes burn fossil fuels such as coal and oil, they pump out carbon dioxide. Burning and cutting down forests also releases carbon dioxide, while farming cattle and rice produces methane, another greenhouse gas. Higher levels of greenhouse gases are overheating Earth.

The last three decades have all broken heat records. Scientists say temperatures have risen by 1.4°F since 1900 and may rise by another 3–12°F by 2100. That may not sound a lot—but temperatures were only 40°F colder during the last ice age! The warming would have a big effect.

3-second sum-up

Air pollution is making Earth overheat.

3-minute mission How a greenhouse works

You need: • 2 thermometers • Glass jar • Timer

Place the thermometers in the sunlight for 3 minutes and record their temperatures. Then place the jar over one of the thermometers. Every minute for 10 minutes, check both thermometers. How did the temperature inside the jar change? The jar traps heat like glass in a greenhouse.

Future weather

...in 30 seconds

Global warming sounds great if you live in a cold country. Unfortunately, there's bad news, too—the weather will most likely become wilder. Experts believe there will be more extreme rainfall, making floods more common. Dry regions such as Africa and Australia could get drier, making it even harder for farmers to grow food. As the oceans get warmer, hurricanes could strike less often but become stronger.

Global warming is making ice caps in the Arctic and Antarctica melt. Ocean water also expands as it warms, which is making sea levels rise. In the future, low-lying coasts around the world, where many large cities are located, could be affected by flooding. If sea levels continue to rise, entire islands could be lost to the waves.

Because sea levels are rising faster than before, many countries are now building sea defenses to stop high waters from flooding coastal cities.

But the real solution is to reduce our use of fossils fuels, and turn to alternative green energy sources that don't cause pollution. These include solar and hydroelectric power. Using electric trains and cars that run on green energy can also help. Solutions like these will help to keep Earth's climate in balance, which will keep wild weather at bay.

3-second sum-up

Using green energy sources can help reduce global warming.

3-minute mission Do your bit

In three minutes, you can reduce the amount of carbon dioxide your family produces in your home.
• Turn down the thermostat on your central heating by 2°F.
• Switch off lights in rooms with no one in them.
• Turn off computers, TVs, and other devices left on standby.
If every family does a little, together we can make a big difference.

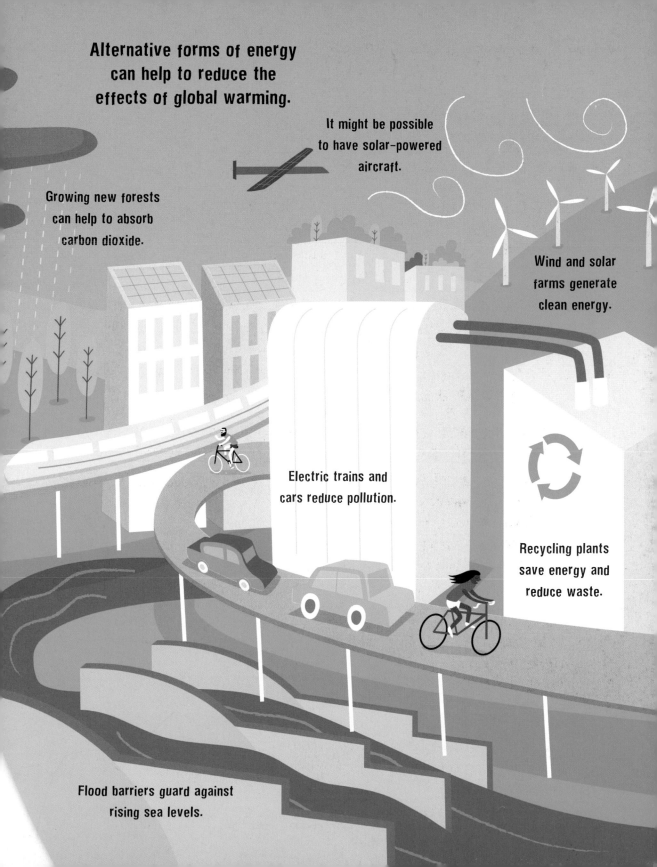

Alternative forms of energy can help to reduce the effects of global warming.

It might be possible to have solar-powered aircraft.

Growing new forests can help to absorb carbon dioxide.

Wind and solar farms generate clean energy.

Electric trains and cars reduce pollution.

Recycling plants save energy and reduce waste.

Flood barriers guard against rising sea levels.

Discover more

NON-FICTION BOOKS

50 Things You Should Know About: Wild Weather by Anna Claybourne
QED Publishing, 2015

Extreme Weather by Ann Squire
C. Press/Franklin Watts Trade, 2014

Eyewitness Activity: Weather Watcher by John Woodward
DK Children, 2015

National Geographic Kids: Everything Weather by Kathy Furgang
National Geographic, 2012

National Geographic Kids: Extreme Weather by Thomas M. Kostigen
National Geographic, 2014

The Everything KIDS' Weather Book by Joe Snedeker, M.Ed.
Adams Media Corporation, 2012

Using the Weather to Learn About Earth by Miriam Coleman
Powerkids Press, 2015

Weather Patterns – The Geography Detective Investigates by Jen Green
Wayland, 2009

DVDs—suitable for all ages

Earth: the Power of the Planet
Introduced by Iain Stewart
Complete BBC Series, 2007

Eyewitness DVD: Weather
Dorling Kindersley, 2006

Show Me Science: How Weather Happens
Allegro Productions, 2012

Wild Weather
Introduced by Donal McIntyre
Complete BBC Series, 2002

WEBSITES

Climate Kids (NASA)
http://climatekids.nasa.gov

Geography4Kids
http://www.geography4kids.com/ files/climate_intro.html

Global Climate Change
http://www.epa.gov/ climatestudents

Hurricane Facts
http://www.sciencekids.co.nz/ sciencefacts/weather/hurricane. html

Weather and Climate
https://sites.google.com/site/ climatetypes/home

World Biomes
http://kids.nceas.ucsb.edu/biomes

Although every endeavor has been made by the publisher to ensure that all content from these websites is educational material of the highest quality and is age appropriate, we strongly advise that Internet access be supervised by a responsible adult.

Quiz answers

Answers to missions on page 28
Polar bear—polar biome
Jaguar—rain forest
Zebra—savannah
Camel—desert

Index

Index